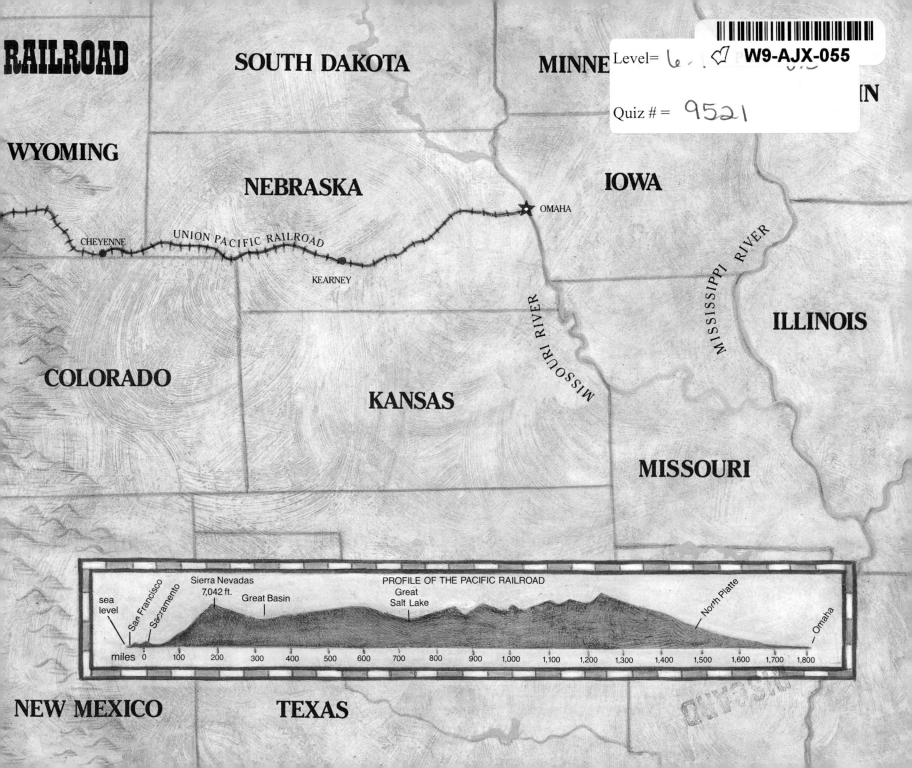

RAILROAD

SOUTH DAKOTA

MINNE

IN

WYOMING

NEBRASKA

IOWA

★ OMAHA

CHEYENNE

UNION PACIFIC RAILROAD

KEARNEY

ILLINOIS

MISSISSIPPI RIVER

MISSOURI RIVER

COLORADO

KANSAS

MISSOURI

PROFILE OF THE PACIFIC RAILROAD

sea
level

Sierra Nevadas
7,042 ft.

Great Basin

Great
Salt Lake

North Platte

Omaha

San Francisco

Sacramento

miles 0   100   200   300   400   500   600   700   800   900   1,000 1,100 1,200 1,300 1,400 1,500 1,600 1,700 1,800

NEW MEXICO   TEXAS

First edition
Published by Henry Holt and Company, Inc.,
115 West 18th Street, New York, New York 10011.
Published simultaneously in Canada
by Fitzhenry & Whiteside Ltd.,
91 Granton Drive, Richmond Hill, Ontario L4B 2N5.

Library of Congress
Cataloging-in-Publication Data
Fraser, Mary Ann.
Ten Mile Day and the building
of the transcontinental railroad /
written and illustrated by Mary Ann Fraser.
Summary: Chronicles the race to build the first
railroad to cross the North American continent.
ISBN 0-8050-1902-2 (alk. paper)
1. Central Pacific Railroad Company —
History — Juvenile literature.
2. Union Pacific Railroad Company —
History — Juvenile literature.
3. Pacific railroads — History —
Juvenile literature.   [1. Railroads —
History.]   I. Title.
HE2791.C455F73   1993
385'.0978 – dc20   92-3007

Printed in the United States of America
on acid-free paper. ∞

1 3 5 7 9 10 8 6 4 2

TEN MILE DAY

AND THE BUILDING OF THE TRANSCONTINENTAL RAILROAD

Written and illustrated by MARY ANN FRASER

Henry Holt and Company

On April 28, 1869, reporters and photographers crawled from their tents into the cold, gray light of early dawn. Soon a small group of officials gathered on a ridge. As daylight spread, workers from rival construction camps jostled for the best view.

The nearly five thousand people who were camped out near the northeast shore of Great Salt Lake, Utah, made a lively and colorful crowd. Businessmen and workers, a military band, and army officers from the nearby garrisons had come to this desolate valley to see the last great push in the building of the first transcontinental railroad – Ten Mile Day.

Theodore Dehone Judah

Theodore Judah was one of the finest railroad engineers of his day. For years he told anyone who would listen that a transcontinental railroad, or Pacific Railroad as he called it, could link east to west. After twenty-three trips through the Sierra Nevadas, he finally surveyed a usable route across the mountains. With the route marked out, he needed to find backers who could pay for the huge construction project.

In 1861 Judah brought together California businessmen Leland Stanford, Charles Crocker, Collis P. Huntington, and Mark Hopkins, later known as the Big Four, to form the Pacific Railroad Company. But even those men did not have enough money, and they had to look to the federal government for help.

The outbreak of the Civil War that same year made Congress see the need for a new rail line to the West Coast. Encouraged by Judah and others, it passed the Pacific Rail Act. On July 1, 1862 President Lincoln signed the act into law.

Once in California again, Judah had many arguments over business practices with his partners. Eventually he decided to return to Washington to regain control of the Central Pacific. On his way east he caught yellow fever and died a few weeks later, on November 2, 1863.

Theodore Judah saw the Pacific Railroad as the means to create a nation. Sixty years after his death a small statue of the man who fought so hard for a transcontinental railroad was erected in Sacramento.

Before the 1860s no railway ran across all of North America, from the Atlantic to the Pacific. Only rough and dangerous wagon roads linked the coasts. Aside from a few local West Coast lines, there were no tracks at all past Omaha, Nebraska, and the ice-capped Sierra Nevadas appeared impassable by rail. But railroad engineer Theodore Dehone Judah was determined to unite east and west with an iron trail. He spent years exploring the Sierras until at last, in 1860, he found the best route across, and through, the mountains.

In 1862, his plan in hand, Judah went to Washington, D.C., to convince Congress it should finance the transcontinental railroad – the greatest engineering feat in American history. The Pacific Railroad Act, which Judah helped to pass, finally made his dream possible, but he died only seven days after the first rails were laid.

Two companies were given the job of building the railroad. To attract investors, the government promised to give money, and even free land, to each company based on the amount of track it laid. The Central Pacific was to begin in Sacramento, California and move east. The Union Pacific would begin in Omaha, Nebraska, and move west. Promontory Summit, Utah, was later chosen as their meeting place.

The Central Pacific and the Union Pacific both broke ground in 1863. As the years went by, leaders of each team began to compete over who could lay the most track in a single day. In the beginning, even one mile a day was difficult. But with experience both companies had become highly skilled and organized. Like a large military campaign, the entire job was broken into smaller tasks, and each task was assigned a crew.

When Charles Crocker, construction boss for the Central Pacific, learned that the Union Pacific had set a new record of seven miles, eighteen hundred feet on October 26, 1868, he boasted that his men could lay ten miles. Dr. Thomas C. Durant, vice president of the Union Pacific, wagered $10,000 that it could not be done.

Most people believed that laying ten miles of track in a day was impossible. But the Central Pacific had already done the impossible many times. In the first years of construction Chinese laborers had blasted fifteen tunnels through the solid granite of the high Sierras. They had overcome dozens of fierce winter blizzards, some with snowdrifts over a hundred feet high, and avalanches that swept away whole crews.

Once past the mountains, the men faced new problems. In the scorching alkali deserts of the Nevada flats, they did not have enough water to drink, and they ran short of building supplies. When the Central Pacific reached Utah, rival Union Pacific crews attacked Chinese workers with pick handles and even detonated explosives near them, killing many.

But Crocker and his crew had learned from their hardships. Now they were an efficient force. As the transcontinental railroad was nearing completion, his army stood ready for its final battle, Ten Mile Day.

Early in the morning of April 28, 1869, Crocker and James Strobridge, his right-hand man, called for volunteers for the difficult task ahead. Each crew was promised four times its normal wages if it could meet the challenge. Nearly all of the team leaders stepped forward. Fourteen hundred of the Central Pacific's best laborers, both Irish and Chinese, were selected out of the almost five thousand volunteers.

The Central Pacific's Labor Force

In 1863, proper Protestants looked down on the Irish, and anti-Chinese feeling ran high. When construction began that same year, the Central Pacific could not find enough laborers. But many Chinese were already at work in California's gold mines. Crocker convinced Strobridge to hire fifty Chinese workers on the railroad, to see how well they would do.

The few hundred white men working for the company did not believe the Chinese were strong enough and resented them for working for less pay. Within a short time, though, Strobridge and the other laborers were forced to admit that the Chinese were good workers. They knew how to work in teams, seldom took breaks, and stayed healthier than the other workers. Still, the whites held on to the skilled jobs and the Chinese were given more dangerous, lower-paying tasks.

Soon Crocker contracted with a San Francisco firm to bring workers directly from Asia. Once in America, the Chinese organized themselves into separate work gangs of twelve to twenty men with their own cooks and bosses. Those who spoke English became the head men, collecting wages and buying supplies for everyone in their crews.

Approximately eleven thousand Chinese, two thousand Irish, and a few African Americans and white Mormons were hired by the Central Pacific to build the transcontinental railroad. Building the line was risky. Almost two thousand Chinese were killed or critically injured by blasting accidents or attacks, avalanches, cholera, or harsh weather conditions.

At 7 A.M. all eyes rested on Charles Crocker as he steadied his horse beside the grade. The crews knew it would take sixteen railroad flatcars to carry everything they needed to lay two miles of track. Five trains, each made up of an engine and sixteen flatcars, now waited. Some stood at the end of the rails and others were parked on the sidings, the tracks built beside the main road. Wooden ties had already been placed along the entire ten mile route. Everything was set to go.

With a sharp command to the bosses, Crocker's arm rose and fell. The hogger, or engineer, on the first train pulled hard on the whistle cord, and a shrill blast pierced the cold, damp morning air. The race had begun.

Chinese laborers leaped onto the flatcars of the lead train. The noise was deafening as sledgehammers knocked out the side stakes and rails tumbled to the ground. The clanging of falling iron continued for eight minutes, until the first sixteen flatcars were empty.

As the supply train was unloaded, three men rushed to the end of the rails, what they called the end o' track. The three pioneers scrambled ahead to the first loose ties. Then they began lifting, prying, and shoving to center the bare ties on the grade.

The emptied train steamed back to the siding, and men hurried to load iron cars with exactly sixteen rails and thirty-two rail joiners, or fishplates, each. A crew of six Chinese workers and an Irish boss hopped aboard.

To the right of the track two horses were hitched by a long rope to an iron car. With a yell from the boss, the horses lurched against their harnesses and the cars rolled forward on the track. When the iron car reached the end o' track, a wooden keg was smashed over the rails. The iron car rambled ahead as new track was laid, spilling spikes through the open bottom and onto the ground where they could be used. Dust clouds choked the air.

With the iron car moving steadily along, eight Irishmen lay rails just ahead of its rolling wheels. These "ironmen" were Michael Shay, Thomas Daley, George Elliot, Michael Sulivan, Edward Killeen, Patrick Joice, Michael Kenedy, and Fred McNamare. The four forward men seized the 560-pound, thirty-foot-long rails, while the four rear men slid the rails to the rollers on each side of the iron car. The lead ironmen ran forward. "Down," shouted the foreman. With a loud thud the iron hit the ties within inches of the previous rail. Without a moment to rest, the eight ironmen went back for more. On average, two rails were laid every twenty seconds.

While rails clanked to the ground, the Chinese crew from the iron car loaded fishplates, nuts, and bolts into baskets attached to poles slung over their shoulders. Then they sped up the line, tossing out ironware every ten yards. Where rail ends met, another team fastened the fishplates loosely with nuts and thrusting bolts.

When each handcar was unloaded, the horses were detached from the front and hitched to the back. At a gallop they hauled the empty iron car back to the supply dump. If a returning car got in the way of a full iron car, the empty one was flipped off the track until the full car passed. Nothing slowed the flow of supplies to the end o' track.

After a track-gauge team measured the rails to insure they were exactly four feet, eight and one half inches apart, the new American and British standard, the rail ends were loosely fastened with fishplates.

Next came the spike setters. Each man picked up one of the spikes lying scattered beside the roadbed, then quickly set it in position with two hits. Another gang of Chinese followed. With three blows from the maul each spike was driven home, securing the rails to the ties.

Some crews had marvelous names. "Fishplate men" tightened the nuts on the thrusting bolts with long-handled wrenches. "Gandy dancers," or "track liners," aligned the rails to the ties using massive track bars. A foreman would sing out a simple tune with a strong beat. Like the crew on a row boat, the gandy dancers would all push together on the final beat, aligning the rails.

Following close on their heels, a surveyor directed a rail gang that lifted the ties and shoveled dirt under them to keep the track level.

The last and largest special work team included four hundred tampers and shovelers. They used crowbars, shovels, and tamping bars to pack the ground around the rails. The crew formed three long lines, one on each side of the track and one down the middle. Each tamper gave two crunching tamps to the gravel, or ballast, before moving on, while shovelers filled in where needed.

From the first pioneer to the last tamper ran a line of men nearly two miles long. Like a mammoth machine with hundreds of well-oiled parts, Crocker's men moved rhythmically forward. The ribbon of track rose across the plain at the pace of a walking man. Tired workers were pulled from the line and replaced. But many, including the eight ironmen, showed no signs of quitting.

The Union Pacific Railroad Company

The Union Pacific, run by Vice President Dr. Thomas C. Durant, did not lay its first pair of rails until July 10, 1865. Delayed by poor organization and a lack of funds, the company only managed to lay a total of forty miles of track that whole year.

The Union Pacific only began to make real progress when Durant hired brothers Jack and Dan Casement and later appointed General Grenville Dodge as chief engineer. Together they organized several thousand Irish, Dutch, Polish, and German immigrants and a small number of African Americans into efficent work crews. By the end of 1866, the men were averaging a mile of track per day.

But the Union Pacific continued to have its share of difficulties. Much of the land west of Omaha was treeless, so timber for ties had to be shipped long distances. The Sioux, Arapaho, and Cheyenne realized that their way of life was threatened by the Iron Horse, and attacked work crews. And the winter of 1867 was the worst on record. Rails had to be laid over the frozen Missouri River to bring supplies across. Fierce blizzards often stopped work. And the heavy spring thaw washed away many miles of track.

Although the Union Pacific also developed specialized work teams, nothing they accomplished compared to the speed and precision of the men of the Central Pacific on Ten Mile Day.

Alongside the grade the telegraph construction party worked frantically to keep pace with the track layers. They set the poles; hammered on the crossbars; and hauled out, hung, and insulated the wire.

The track boss stalked up and down the line, barking out commands and encouragement. The steady hammering of spikes, the rhythmic thud of iron rails, and even the men's labored breathing beat like a drum across the barren plain.

A reporter pulled out his pocket watch and counted the rails as they were laid down. To everyone's amazement 240 feet of iron were placed in one minute and twenty seconds.

By 9 A.M. almost two miles of track had been spiked and tamped. Even the Union Pacific men, who had laughed at the Central Pacific crews, had to admit it was quality work.

Water, food, and tool wagons creaked up and down the line as the heat rose with the morning sun. Chinese workers wove in and out of the men, delivering water and tea to quench their thirst.

At the front Crocker and Strobridge oversaw every detail. Now and then when something amusing happened, Crocker's merry laugh echoed from his carriage.

With the completion of another two miles of track, the second supply train pulled back to the siding and the third train steamed forward, belching thick clouds of black smoke. Next in line, ready to serve the midday meal, was the so-called Pioneer Train – the boarding house for some of the workers, and the office and living quarters of James and Hannah Strobridge.

At 1:30 the whistle sounded, calling a halt for lunch. Whirlwind No. 62, the Pioneer Train locomotive, pushed the kitchen cars up, and the boarding boss served hot boiled beef.

A quick measurement showed that six miles of track had already been laid, spiked, and bolted that morning. Whoops and hollers went up as the news spread among the men. They were now confident they could reach their goal of ten miles in one day, and they named their rest stop Camp Victory.

The Pioneer Train

The Central Pacific's Pioneer Train, pulled by the locomotive called Whirlwind No. 62, was like a small town on wheels. A car on one end of the train was James and Hannah Strobridge's home and office, complete with fine furnishings, an awning, and a canary cage swinging from the front door. When a wire was run to the poles nearby, the car became an instant telegraph office.

Hannah Strobridge, the "Heroine of the Central," traveled with her husband aboard the Pioneer Train. She was the only woman to see the Central Pacific build the railroad from start to finish.

Coupled to the Strobridges' car was the boarding house. It was a long line of wooden houses built on flatcars. In the houses were sleeping quarters for five hundred men.

The Pioneer Train also included kitchen cars. At midday and again in the evenings, the train was moved to the end of the track to serve the men their meals.

At 2:30 work began again, but a special crew had to be called in. The tracks were now climbing the west slope of the Promontory Mountains. The climb was steep and full of curves, and the rails had to be bent.

Lacking measuring instruments, this new crew judged the curves by sight. They jammed the rails between blocks and then slowly and carefully hammered them into the right shapes. Every rail now took extra time to mold and fit.

As the afternoon wore on, the foreman continued to ride the line, encouraging the men. Although the horses pulling the iron cars were changed every two hours, they could no longer run up the grade. Now they had to walk slowly up the steep hillside. The rail gang was dripping with sweat, and their muscles must have burned from overuse, but not one man stopped to rest. With each hour another mile of track reached toward Promontory Summit.

By 7 P.M. the sun was dipping behind Monument Point. Strobridge signaled for the final blast from the train whistle. The exhausted men cast down their tools, and the day's work came to an abrupt end.

How much rail had the men of the Central Pacific laid? Two Union Pacific engineers took out their surveying chains and began to measure. Everyone waited for the final count. Then it came. The railhead was ten miles, fifty-six feet farther east than it had been the previous evening.

The crews flung their hats into the air, cheering and shaking hands all around. They had done the impossible again. The Union Pacific's record was destroyed, and Thomas Durant lost the bet. A total of 3,520 rails, twice that number of fishplates, 28,160 spikes, and 14,080 nuts and bolts had been placed to complete the job.

The eight track layers were declared heroes and were featured in later histories.

Each had lifted over 125 tons of iron. No single crew has ever beaten their record. The Chinese workers had once again proven themselves to their biased rivals. Each team had something to celebrate.

Crocker called for one of his locomotives to test the track. The train roared over the line at up to forty miles an hour, setting the rails and proving the job well done. Pushed by two engines, the fifth and last emptied supply train backed down the mountain with the weary yet jubilant men riding its flatcars.

The Central Pacific's end o' track was now only four miles from Promontory Summit. The Union Pacific had nine and a half miles of track left to lay. By May 9 all of the remaining rails were in place except two. The momentous joining of the transcontinental railroad would take place 1,086 miles west of the Missouri River and 690 miles east of Sacramento.

The Golden Spike

Wealthy San Franciscan David Hewes was so excited about the completion of the transcontinental railroad that he commissioned a golden spike to be used on the very last rail. The spike included the following inscriptions on its four sides:

1. The names and titles of the Central Pacific officers.
2. The names and titles of the Central Pacific directors. (The Union Pacific officers were left out.)
3. "The Pacific Railroad – Ground broken Jany 8th 1863; completed May 8th 1869." (Though the spike stated that the final day would be the eighth, the ceremony did not actually take place until the tenth.)
4. "May God continue the unity of our Country as the Railroad unites the two great Oceans of the world. Presented by David Hewes, San Francisco."

On the head of the spike itself was the inscription: "The Last Spike."

A large nugget was left attached to the spike, to be broken off and made into souvenirs after the ceremony.

Three other special spikes were also used at the Promontory Summit ceremony, including another golden spike provided by a newspaper company. But Hewes's spike, which had the most real gold in it, became known as the "Golden Spike."

At eleven o'clock on the bright, brisk morning of May 10, 1869, several hundred people gathered at Promontory Summit. Eight Chinese in new blue jackets laid the final pair of rails. Four spikes, two of them made of gold, were set into a polished California laurelwood tie. Leland Stanford, president of the Central Pacific; Thomas Durant; and several other officials then ceremoniously tapped them with a silver-headed maul.

Immediately Chinese workers removed the four glittering spikes and the laurel tie. Three iron spikes were then driven into a pine tie. A telegraph wire was secured to the head of a fourth iron spike and another wire connected to the head of an iron maul so the nation could "hear" the spike driven home.

Clunk. Stanford missed, hitting the tie. The telegrapher tapped out three dots anyway, signaling "done" to the rest of the world. Durant then stepped forward to strike the spike. He didn't even hit the tie! A regular rail worker eventually hammered the spike into place.

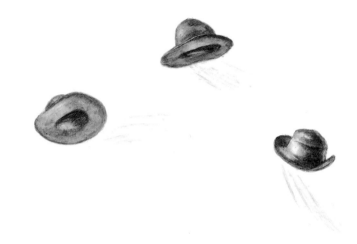

From Sacramento to Washington, D.C., bells rang in celebration. Cheering people filled the streets. Guns and cannons were fired into the air.

The two engines moved toward each other until their pilots nearly touched over the last rail. Above the din of rousing cheers and whistles of locomotives, Durant shook Stanford's hand, declaring, "There is henceforth but one Pacific Railroad of the United States." Theodore Judah's dream of a transcontinental railroad was now a reality.

The Next Day...and Beyond

Completed a full year ahead of schedule and five years ahead of most expectations, the Pacific Railroad quickly began to change the face of the nation.

On May 11, 1869, one day after the Golden Spike ceremony, the first train bound for the west steamed into Promontory Summit. Soon the era of covered wagons was at an end. In its place came a rapidly expanding rail system capable of delivering freight and passengers across the country in six to seven days.

In their race to finish the job and begin making money, though, the builders of both railroad companies were guilty of much poor workmanship. The Central Pacific eventually made repairs, but the Union Pacific was very slow in mending its tracks and bridges. Neither company made as much money from the line as they had hoped.

In 1860 thirteen million bison roamed the prairies. But as the railroad moved west it brought hunters who slaughtered the animals with terrible efficiency. By the end of the century only a few hundred of the great beasts remained. Gone with them was the livelihood of the native peoples of the plains. The U.S. government gave away the Native Americans' land to the settlers and miners brought by the trains. The native peoples protested and fought bitterly, but their struggle was in vain. In the end they were driven onto reservations. Only today are the courts reconsidering some of their claims.

Though it brought an end to the native peoples' way of life, the railroad also made possible the nation we live in today. Graduates of training schools set up by the Union Pacific and the Central Pacific helped to build four more transcontinental railroads. On those tracks came millions of Americans and immigrants, all seeking a better way of life. Farms and ranches began to dot the landscape. Soon towns grew up and local governments were formed. In 1912 the last of the forty-eight contiguous states joined the union. For better or worse, the transcontinental railroad *had* united the nation.

Acknowledgments

The more research I did for this book, the more contradictions I encountered. I became a detective trying to unravel the events of Ten Mile Day and the building of the transcontinental railroad. Sometimes, when sources clashed and experts disagreed, I simply had to make my own choices. For example, the names of the eight ironmen who laid the rails on Ten Mile Day are spelled differently in every source and study. I chose to use the names as they appear on the paymaster's sheet for April 28, 1869. Readers are sure to see alternate spellings in other books.

There were some questions, though, that none of my books or

documents could answer. Researching those problems led me to many places, including the 1991 Railfair in Sacramento, the Orange Empire Railway Museum, and the California State Library.

When illustrating this book, I tried to obtain visual information from photographs whenever possible. I wanted my art to accurately represent Ten Mile Day and to acknowledge the workers' individual efforts. The eight ironmen who laid the track, however, fail to appear in any photographs, and although the Chinese made up ninety percent of the Central Pacific's labor force, they were seldom photographed. I am grateful to the Asian-American Studies Department at the University of California, Los Angeles, for confirming that some of the Chinese laborers rolled their queues under their hats while working and others did not.

The real end of my quest for answers came at the Golden Spike Historic Site. There, I photographed the tools used by the workers and replicas of the locomotives. Riding in a pick-up truck over the remnants of the Central Pacific's grade, I saw firsthand the scenes of Ten Mile Day and the joining of the rails.

For their assistance and enthusiasm during my research, I wish to thank Randy Kane and Monte Crooks of the Golden Spike Historic Site; Walter P. Gray III, Curator of the California State Railroad Museum; and the Orange Empire Railway Museum.

Suggested Reading

Best, Gerald M. *Iron Horses to Promontory*. San Marino, Calif.: Golden West Books, 1969; written for adults.

Brown, Dee. *Lonesome Whistle*. New York: Holt, Rinehart, and Winston, 1980; adapted for young readers from the useful adult book, *Hear That Lonesome Whistle Blow*.

Griswold, Wesley S. *Work of Giants*. New York: McGraw Hill, 1962; a well researched adult account.

Krauss, George. *High Road to Promontory: Building the Central Pacific Across the High Sierras*. Palo Alto, Calif.: American West, 1969; one of the best books on the Central Pacific, but aimed at adult readers.

Latham, Frank B. *The Transcontinental Railroad 1862–69: A Great Engineering Feat Links America Coast to Coast*. New York: Franklin Watts, 1973; an illustrated book for younger readers.

Miller, Marilyn. *The Transcontinental Railroad*. Morristown, N.J.: Silver Burdett, 1986; illustrated with photographs, for younger readers.

Stein, R. Conrad. *The Story of the Golden Spike*. Chicago: Children's Press, 1978; illustrated introduction for younger readers.

Williams, John Hoyt. *A Great and Shining Road*. New York: Times Books, 1988; aimed at adult readers, useful for extensive footnotes to original sources.

Glossary

ballast: gravel or rocks used to hold ties in place and to provide good drainage.

couple: to hook two train cars together.

end o' track: the railhead, or end of the tracks.

engineer: 1. a driver of a train. 2. a person who designs and directs construction of a railroad.

fishplate: a flat piece of metal used to connect two rails end-to-end.

flatcar: a railroad car without any sides.

gandy dancer: a man who aligns the rails; also called a track liner.

gang: a crew of railroad workers.

grade: ground that has been leveled and smoothed for a railroad.

hogger: the engineer, or driver of a train; also called a hoggie, or hoghead.

iron car: a flat car pulled over rails by men or animals, used to carry iron rails, tools, and supplies.

Iron Horse: the Native Americans' name for a locomotive.

ironmen: the men who lay the rails onto the ties.

maul: a hammer for driving spikes.

pioneer: a person who aligns the ties.

rail: an iron bar forming a train track.

roadbed: the ground upon which the rails, ties, and ballast rest.

siding: a set of tracks running alongside the main tracks.

spike: a large nail for securing the rails to the ties.

surveyor: a person who measures the land to determine the route for the railroad.

tamper: a person who packs down the ballast.

thrusting bolt: a pin used to secure a fishplate to a rail.

tie: the wooden supports to which rails are fastened.